A Call to Surrender

Jamie Womack

A Call to Surrender

Author: Jamie Womack

Published by Austin Brothers Publishing

Fort Worth, Texas

www.austinbrotherspublishing.com

ISBN 978-0-9903477-0-5

Copyright © 2014 by Jamie Womack

Austin Brothers
Publishing

Cover Design by Jay Cookingham

This and other books published by Austin Brothers Publishing can be purchased at www.austinbrotherspublishing.com

Printed in the United States of America

2012 -- First Edition

I would like to dedicate this book to my

Lord and Savior Jesus Christ

who orchestrated the events, people, trials, and triumphs in my life in such a way that

He has woven the beauty of compassion, grace, and forgiveness in the midst of brokeness.

These are the principles upon which

He has built the ministry of my testimonial message "A Call To Surrender."

I would like to also dedicate this book to

my husband Jimmy

who is my soul mate and partner in Christ.

He has stood by me and supported me whole heartedly. His godly wisdom has proven

to be that of righteousness in many situations.

Jimmy is the joy of my life and my miracle.

Contents

Contents

Foreword

Be an Encourager!

There is an ungodly characteristic frequently found in Christian circles. It is the lack of encouragement in our relationship with others. It is almost epidemic! When was it essential the last time you encouraged someone else? I believe that a Christian is never more Christ-like than when full of compassion for the discouraged.

Listen to this silent cry of one without any encouragement.

I cry tears to you my Lord, because I cannot speak.

Words are lost among my fears, pain, sorrows, losses, hurts, but tears You understand. My wordless prayer You hear.

Lord, wipe away my tears, all tears not in distant day, but, now, here!

If you have shaped the words silently in your mind, "Encourage Me."

If you are looking for encouragement and found it in short supply, this book is for you. Jamie opens her heart and shares her life of discouragement, and how she decided to offer her pain, disappointments, and discouragement to the Lord, to use as He would see fit. Even in the midst of emotional trauma, she has persevered and found total and complete fulfilment in allowing our Lord to use her challenges for His Glory. Jamie became an ENCOURAGER. God has opened the doors to thousands who have received her encouragement to them.

Gary Mitchell
Bivo/Smaller Church Specialist
Louisiana Baptists

Jamie Womack

A Miraculous Beginning

During the early 1970's, my parents along with my three sisters moved to Oklahoma City, OK. My dad served on staff as Minister of Outreach at Putnam City Baptist Church. Since they were new in town, my dad made an all out effort to search for the best hospital and the best doctor for Mom to give birth to their fourth daughter. As you will see, man's best efforts can never override the plans of a Sovereign God.

It was Sunday night, May 20, 1973, the night the life of Jamie Susanne Chaney on earth began. As my mom was waiting to go into delivery, she told the nurse that something did not feel right. This was Mom's forth time to give birth, so she knew the way she felt was not normal. By the time the doctor arrived in the delivery room, things had already gone array. I was in breach position, which caused the cord that connected to my mother's womb to be wrapped around my neck. Therefore, my oxygen circulation was cut off. Doctors immediately hooked me up to a respirator. I did not take a breath on my own for the first thirty-two minutes of life.

Doctors predicted the worst. They said that if I did survive the night, which was questionable, I would be nothing more than a vegetable. Furthermore, they recommended to my father that he should put me into an institution as soon as possible. Fortunately, I have Christian parents who believe in the sanctity of life. Therefore, Dad immediately said no to that recommendation, knowing that God had other plans for his daughter's life.

I remained on the respirator overnight. The next morning they were able to take me off. During the next few days, I experienced trembling and seizures. It was also difficult for me to suck in order to eat. I stayed in the hospital for eight days.

God miraculously intervened and freed me totally from any mental damage or mental retardation. He placed his sovereign protective hand on the mental capacity of my brain. However, the part of my brain that controls my muscles was severely damaged. Each step of physical progress was slow, challenging, but a tiny miracle.

Over the first couple of years it was apparent that my physical development would be delayed. The simple things such as head control and sitting up were a challenge. At one year old I was not walking yet. When I was 15 months old,

I was diagnosed with cerebral palsy. Cerebral palsy basically means I am unable to control my muscles as much as I would like. I began to walk when I was two.

My parents put me in a preschool for children with special needs. It was there that I received intense therapy. The preschool director was named Mr. Chip. I still remember being in the swimming pool and working with a lady with blonde hair. She made therapy fun. Progress was slow, but I was able to master the basic things of life. I began to walk at the age of two.

During my primary school years, I had various therapists. We lived in Muskogee, OK, for a couple of years. I attended the CP Center where Pat Pack was the head therapist. In the summer before my first grade year, we moved to Lafayette, LA. The Lafayette Parish School System had an excellent program where therapists were at the schools. Therefore, my therapy sessions were incorporated into my school day. The therapists in Lafayette made a lasting impression. They were genuinely nice people who not only did therapy but talked to me with normal conversations.

One of them was Ms. Gerry. She was my speech therapist during first and second grades. Ms. Gerry made speech therapy fun. We would often sit and play the card game "Fish." As we played, she would do speech with me. That provided fun interaction and one-on-one attention that would be meaningful to me. I believe her personal relational skills set the stage for her to be there for me in a specific situation.

One day I was scheduled to go to speech at the end of the day. This particular day it was very upsetting to me because it was my turn to wash the chalkboard. To a second grader, washing the chalkboard is a big deal. I was going to miss that because I was required to attend speech. It aroused the emotional struggle within me of just wanting to be like the other kids.

When I arrived at speech, Ms. Gerry could tell I was really upset. We ended up just talking that day. I recall her having the deck of cards in her hands. She just kept shuffling the cards and simply listened to my heart. She understood what was going on inside of me. That meant the world to me.

Through therapy during my early years, I was able to master the ability to do most things that would enable me to live a normal life. I remember learning to tie a shoe and pour milk. It was a struggle, but I did it. Ms. Debra was my occupational therapist. She had me practice typing to strengthen my fingers. I confess that was one thing I did not enjoy. Nevertheless, Ms. Debra was cool. I recall sitting on her lap and practicing buttoning a vest on her. Again, that one-on-one interaction was what meant so much.

The only time that I really suffered physically was when I was in seventh grade. It was on a Monday night. I was standing at the kitchen counter at home. While I was pouring a glass of milk, a sharp pain went through my back. My leg tightened and contracted to the point that I could not straighten it. My sister Janet, who ran track and was very athletic, had to carry me to the couch.

Over the next two months, I experienced excruciating back pain. The only time I was not in pain was when I was laying down perfectly still. Walking became a tremendous battle. One day at school, I was walking out to recess. As I came parallel to the fence, my legs buckled under the pain and I crumbled to the ground. Being in agonizing pain, I knew that if I pulled up on the fence, I would not be able to bend down and get my books. I felt totally helpless. So I sat there during recess and prayed that someone would come help me.

After recess, the bell rang and everyone was walking to go back to class. A girl named Kelli Yarbrough saw me and came to help. I asked if she would hand me my books if I pulled myself up by the fence. She compassionately went a step further and walked with me and carried my books.

That incident has always stuck in my mind because Kelli's simple act of kindness during one of my most desperate times meant so much. I often thought of Kelli through the years and wished I could just say thank you once again for being there for me that day. Lo and behold, God gave me that opportunity when I connected with her on *Facebook* a couple of years ago.

During that time, my parents wondered about the cause of my back pain. We never pinpointed the cause. The fear of having to be put in a wheelchair was very real. I went to a chiropractor and it did help some, but the pain was lingering. Dad asked the staff members at church to pray for me. I know that it was through the power of prayer that God delivered me from the pain after a couple of months.

Perhaps the greatest physical obstacle as a kid came when I was sixteen. I was faced with the possibility of never being able to drive a car. To most teenagers, this would have been devastating. However, I had a contentment that I know only God can give. I was honest before God and said, "Lord, if you can glorify yourself through me not having a license then let it be." Two years later He honored that contentment and I did receive my license.

God has blessed me beyond measure physically. However, the emotional trauma has been great. In the following chapters, I will take you into the chambers of my heart where emotional battles have been fought and victories have been won through Jesus Christ.

Spiritual Beginnings

I was blessed to grow up in a Christian home. Dad was a Baptist minister and Mom was a music teacher. Naturally being a Christian minister's daughter, church was a prominent part of life. We were trained to attend church every time the doors were open. I remember being asked to a slumber party on a Saturday night. Mom said I could go for a little while but would not be allowed spend the night because of church. How grateful I am for that legacy of going to church.

When I was five, Dad accepted the call to be the Minister of Outreach at FBC, Lafayette, Louisiana. It was spring of 1979, when our family flew to Lafayette for our first visit. The pastor, Rev. Perry Sanders, picked us up in the red church van. I recall Bro. Perry's friendly and welcoming spirit. That set the tone for what I would experience in Lafayette.

FBC, Lafayette became a place of spiritual beginnings for me starting with the tremendous portrayal of God's love through the people. They embraced me with unconditional love and acceptance. Within the first few Sundays that we were there, a man told me that he wanted me in his Sunday School class. I had no idea who he was. So I told Dad that some man wants me in his class. Dad found out who taught 5-year-olds in Sunday School, and figured out it was Mr. Charlie White. That memory has always stuck out in my mind because Mr. Charlie took the initiative to reach out to me and make feel included.

Adults and kids alike welcomed me in as one of them. I was treated with equal respect as everyone else. All of the leaders had a genuine kindred and loving spirit. This created joy and excitement in me about going to church. I enjoyed the people so much.

Bro. Perry was one of the godliest people I have ever known. He was a fire and brimstone preacher. He knew what God's Word said and did not waver from the truth. Bro. Perry preached with a fierceness and boldness that was so inspiring and influential to both young and old. He had a heart for the gospel and for all to know Jesus. His zeal for witnessing was contagious to the whole congregation. *Evangelism Explosion* and *Continuing Witness Training* classes were constantly in session. My dad was in charge of leading them.

One night Bro. Perry went with my family to another church for an associational meeting. He preached on Heaven that night. It was so passionate and heart-felt. I knew that the passion for that sermon came from one of the most heart-breaking experiences of his life--losing his wife to cancer just a few weeks prior to that service. It had such an impact because it was a prime example of living out God's Word even in the midst of the storms of life.

Outside the pulpit, he knew how to relate to people. He did little things such as pass out coins to the kids at church. Even in a large church, he sent out birthday cards. When I was seven, I had to make a trip back to Oklahoma for my uncle to perform eye surgery on me. After spending the night in the hospital, my family stayed with my aunt and uncle. The telephone rang and my cousin answered. He looked at me and said it was for me. I was shocked because I never got phone calls at home much less on a trip. Lo and behold, it was Bro. Perry calling to check on me. Having Bro. Perry as my childhood pastor was definitely a priceless treasure.

The leaders were also godly. Sunday School teachers, choir directors, and Training Union teachers had incredible insight into God's Word. Godly principles were taught from young to old. I remember first grade Training Union where Mrs. Melva Scott taught me what it meant to forgive. In fourth through sixth grades I was in Bible Drill where we memorized countless verses from God's Word. In seventh grade, Mrs. Patsy Methvin was my Sunday School teacher.

One thing that really stood out was the seriously intent look on her face as she taught the Word of Life to us. Because of the leaders' love for me and love for God's teachings, God created in me a deep love for His people and His Word.

I accepted Christ when I was six. My dad baptized me. I really believe that I was saved at that point. One of the main reasons is because I had a longing for spiritual things and to know God. My dad reminds me of a time when I was eleven. He and I were riding in the car. He asked me how I knew that I was saved. I said that my spirit bears witness with His spirit. That stems from the passage found in Romans 8:14-16:

> For those who are led by the Spirit of God are the children of God. The Spirit you received does not make you slaves, so that you live in fear again; rather, the Spirit you received brought about your adoption to sonship. And by him we cry, "Abba, Father." The Spirit himself testifies with our spirit that we are God's children

However, throughout the next several years, I struggled with doubts of my salvation. It was not until I lived in Oklahoma my eighth grade year that God would settle this for me. I was at a Dawson McAllister youth conference. Bro. Dawson was speaking about the cross. It was as if I had never heard it before although I had heard it all my life. I prayed the sinner's prayer again. I felt assurance that I was a child of the King! I went ahead and got baptized again the next night at my church just to make sure I had done it in the right order - salvation then baptism.

A couple of years ago, I received a message on *Facebook* from a teenager who had heard me speak that night at her church. She said that she had been saved as a young child, but as she heard me speak, it was like a light bulb came on in her heart. God was just reaffirming her salvation. As I shared my story with her, she was excited to know that I had a similar experience. The salvation experience is the single most important decision in life for it determines our eternal destiny.

Internal Wars

The setting was our family living room. It was a typical night when our family had friends over for dinner and fellowship. The adults were in the other room and all the kids were in the living room. I was about eight at the time. We were playing card games and having a good time.

One of the card games we played was called "Spoon." To play "Spoon," all the players sat in a circle with spoons placed in the center. The number of spoons depended on the number of players. There was one less spoon than the number of players. We combined two decks of cards. Each player received four cards for his or her hand. One player took the rest of the cards and passed one card at a time to all the players. As the players looked at each card, the object was to get four matching cards such as four 7's, four 8's, etc. When a player had four matching cards, he would quietly grab one of the spoons. When the rest of the players noticed, we raced to grab a spoon. One player was left without a spoon and therefore out of the game. Several hands were played until only one person was left and won the game.

It wasn't very far into the game that I was the one left without a spoon. That really upset me. I remember running upstairs to my room crying. My dad heard me from the other room and followed me upstairs. He just wanted to see if I was okay. It was as if he knew what was going through my heart and mind and that I did not need to be corrected at that moment.

On the surface, I probably appeared to be a spoiled little kid who got upset because I lost a game. However, the struggle that was going on inside of me that night was much different and deeper. It was a struggle that I believe is embedded inside every child who has normal mental capabilities yet struggles with the limitations of a physical disability. It is like a war filled with feelings of inadequacies and insecurities inside a child who is striving to keep up with a society that can function at a faster pace.

Since the nature of the game "Spoon" was speed, that internal struggle was manifest as we played. In my mind I knew what to do and how to do things; yet I was unable to get my muscles to move and function to normal capacity. Over time, frustration builds up so that in certain situations when I came face to face with the reality that I could not function as quickly as other kids, emotions arose. This pressure on a child's heart is very great.

Another instance happened that year when again I was faced with the reality that I was slower than everyone else. This time it was at school. We all know about speed tests in math. Normally I was given extra time. But this one particular day, the speed test really got to me. I remember being upset in the hallway. This guy named Archie in my class came out to talk to me. He was very encouraging to me. It was people like Archie who simply talked to me and listened to me during my times of frustrations who made a lasting impression on me.

On into the next year as I entered the 4th grade, a big thing at church for 4th through 6th graders was Bible Drill. Bible Drill was an excellent tool to train kids in Scripture memorization. We also learned the books of the Bible as well as key passages. At the end of the school year we would be involved in three competitions. The competitions included Scripture quotation and Scripture search. There was a time limit of 10 seconds.

Once again, time and speed became an obstacle for me. The Scripture quotation part was no problem. God blessed me with the ability to memorize quickly and efficiently. However, the Scripture search part was just absolutely terrifying to me because it did involve finding passages of Scripture in ten seconds. I remember thinking there's just no way that I'm going to be able to do well in the competitions.

On the first Sunday after Christmas holidays when we started drilling for competition, the pressure became too much. I went to my dad's office. I sat on his lap and he listened to his daughter's tears of frustration. I said things such as, "Dad, it hurts. It's not fair." That night will forever be in my memory because my dad held me and simply listened.

My mom and dad did talk to the Bible Drill Director who was already thinking of accommodations. She was a very gracious lady named Rose Knight. As we worked through the situation, we came up with a ten second time extension as well as a table on which to place my Bible. These simple accommodations enabled me to be very successful during the three years that I was in Bible Drill. In fact, I recently chatted with a girl on *Facebook* who was in Bible Drill with me. She reminded me that I eventually got to where I was finding Scriptures faster than everyone else and did not need the time extension.

It is interesting to me that God led me to write about the three previous situations for several reasons. First of all, each situation occurred in a different environment - home, school, and church. At that time in life, those were the three main places that I went to. It showed that no matter where I was that internal struggle of wanting to be able to function and be like everybody else was constantly in my mind and heart. That is human nature for anyone. So when the manifestations of those struggles are aroused inside a child's heart through certain situations, frustrations occur.

Another reason of interest was because the struggle was internal, not external. In all three situations there was no one putting pressure on me. I was in settings where I felt very comfortable with the people surrounding me. In fact, in the Bible Drill occurrence, accommodations were already in the process of being made. My third grade teacher was one of the most understanding teachers I ever had. Still, there was that internal drive and desire to just be able to do things like everyone else.

These internal struggles increased as I got older. In the following pages, I will share how they created real fear in me in having access to life opportunities. This war is very real inside the heart of a person with a disability. God used Dad and Archie to give me what I needed most during those moments of frustrations—a listening ear.

Social Barriers

From the onset of social experiences, I began to face the harsh realities of the social barriers that children with special needs encounter. These barriers include being teased and ridiculed or just being left out.

My earliest recollection of being singled out happened when I was only five. I was at a birthday party. All the kids were getting ready to play a game. One little girl said, "Everyone can play but her." She pointed her finger right at me. I remember standing out in the hallway by myself. Amazingly, 36 years later, I still remember that little girl's face.

Instances that may seem so trivial to the world, yet to the child with special needs, it is very traumatic. I knew it was because I was different. Throughout my elementary school days, I got teased because of the way I walk and talk. This created a lot of insecure feelings. The inward struggle to feel equal to other kids was very intense and real.

The social barriers at school would create yet another reason that FBC, Lafayette would become one of the most special places to me. The people there overwhelmed me with unconditional love and acceptance. It became my safe haven. When I felt left out at school, I knew I could go to church and escape in the love of the people. God used FBC to be a tremendous comfort and support system during those primary years. And I needed that. As a little child, just the shunning created the feelings of being harder to accept and therefore like and love. The enormous love that I felt at church ministered to me in such a powerful way.

For my fifth grade year my parents sent me to a private Christian school. Since Christians had been my safe haven, I assumed that this would be like church and that I would be readily accepted. Unfortunately, my assumptions proved to be painfully wrong. The teasing and the ridicule got so bad that I was not able to even finish the school year out. I completed my work at home.

I was homeschooled my sixth grade year. You would think that because I was homeschooled that year, I would have been active in all of the activities at church. However, I found myself shutting down socially. For the first time, I stayed out of choir and Sunday School for the entire year. I spent that time in my dad's office. I just really did not want to be around people much. That was my last year in Bible Drill so it was the one thing I did participate in. It just goes to show how much of an effect that social barriers can have on a child with special needs.

Jamie Womack

During that same year, FBC, Lafayette called a new youth minister. His name was Bro. Paul Strahan. From the start, Bro. Paul befriended me. He really got me motivated again to get involved in church activities again as I promoted in the youth group in seventh grade. Bro. Paul made a profound statement to me that has always stuck with me. He said, "God does not make junk. He makes no mistakes. He made you the way you are special for His Kingdom."

At the beginning of my eighth grade year, my family moved back to Oklahoma. This was extremely difficult for me emotionally. It was hard because I had to leave FBC, Lafayette which had become my security and comfort zone. FBC was where I learned to love God's people. It was also the place where I was taught to love His Word. As I will discuss later, it was from that church that I met two of my dearest friends who impacted my life for Christ the most.

Beginning in eighth grade and going through high school, I attended a Christian school. Again, I thought things would be good socially since it was a Christian school. And again, my thoughts proved to be wrong. The kind of teasing and ridicule that I faced was unlike I had ever known. Previously, I had only dealt with the teasing of my disability. Through teasing in high school, the kids attacked and distorted my personal character. What started out as teasing turned into serious attacks on my character. It was even carried out as far as printing something very destructive about my character in the school newspaper.

The bullying in high school took a great emotional toll on me. I became emotionally timid as I realized it would be an everyday struggle to be accepted and respected in society. Life was a constant emotional struggle. There were many days that I struggled to get out of bed.

The day before my junior year was to begin, my older sister Julie saw me really struggle emotionally just to get enough strength to go to school the next day. I went to bed that night and got up the next morning to get ready for school. When I went to get my binder, I found that Julie had taped an index card to the front of my binder. On it she had written, "Casting all your cares upon Him for He cares for you. 1 Peter 5:7." For you see, Julie knew I was at one of those low points in life that I needed a verse from God's Word to hold on to.

Teasing is a subject not to be taken lightly. It has severe effects and leaves lasting scars. In my ministry, I have had adults come up to me and share their stories of being teased and bullied in school. I can see the pain in their faces as they talk about the scars they still carry. One man came up to me and said that many of his wounds from being teased were opened as I talked about my experiences. How ironic that God would turn one of the most painful childhood trials and use it as a tool to minister to the deep scars of others.

Jamie Womack

My Angel From Heaven

"When Jesus walked on the earth, people were drawn to Him because of His love, warmth, compassion, and His mercy. Today, they will be drawn to Him, through you, the same way." Dr. Jerry Pipes

One day I read the above quote on *Facebook* and could not think of a more fitting quote to begin this chapter. Dr. Jerry Pipes describes the very reason why I got close to a particular person. It was during my sixth grade year when I had shut down socially, I started to observe a lady at church. Although I had known her all through the years, she just really caught my eye that year. The lady's name was Mrs. Betty Best. She was one of the deacon's wives. While we were there, she became the Preschool Director. I never had her as a teacher, which will tell you just how powerful her life witness was on my life, just through a child's observation.

I began to notice Mrs. Betty's warm gentle compassionate spirit. It was radiant, genuine, and transparent—unlike I had ever seen. I was in complete awe of how warm and loving Mrs. Betty was. She showered tender loving compassion and grace to everyone around her. Her warm disposition truly glowed as the radiance of Christ. Luke 4:22 says, "And all spoke well of him and marveled at the gracious words that were coming from his mouth . . ." I remember just marveling at Ms. Betty's warm and loving spirit.

To a kid that struggled emotionally in life, that looked really good. One Wednesday night at church supper, I went up to her and her husband Mr. Terry. I gave them one of my school pictures. They both embraced me with an unbelievable love and compassion. That night sparked a forever friendship with Mr. Terry and Mrs. Betty.

From that point on, I could hardly wait to get to church to see Mrs. Betty. I remember sitting in the gym at Wednesday night supper and just watching and waiting for Mrs. Betty to come in. As soon as I saw her from a distance, my heart would warm. I knew when I got close, she would embrace me with so much love and compassion. Ms. Betty always gave me the feeling that I was someone special and precious in her sight. I felt a very deep genuine compassion and affection that literally felt like heaven to the heart of a child who had to struggle so much emotionally with life.

Jamie Womack

One night at Wednesday night prayer meeting, I went to sit by Mrs. Betty. I sat by her just so I could feel her warm gentle compassionate spirit throughout the service. I remember her placing her hand on my hymn book to help me with the pages. Looking up into her eyes, I saw such gentleness and compassion, as of the sweet aroma of Christ. "For we are the aroma of Christ to God among those who are being saved and among those who are perishing." 2 Corinthians 2:15

Leaving Mrs. Betty was the hardest part about moving. However, distance created avenues for Mrs. Betty and me to become extremely close. We corresponded with each other through letters. Her letters so eloquently reflected her deep gentle love and compassion that she had for me. That enabled me to freely share my heartfelt feelings with her. Mrs. Betty's letters were such a comfort to me as I was going through the emotional struggles of high school.

Because our family had lived in Lafayette for so long, we went back about once a year to visit. I would always surprise Ms. Betty. She would have the most excited and joyous look on her face when she saw me. She always had her tender loving arms open wide ready to embrace me. I valued those few moments each year so much. Her warm gentle compassion went deep into my heart and soul. God used Mrs. Betty to minister to me in a very unique and and powerful way. I just loved her so much. She touched my heart in ways that it has never been touched.

There were so many special memories that Mrs. Betty and I shared. I recall being in her office one day when I was visiting. We were talking and all of a sudden, she asked me, "How are your legs? Do they hurt?"

It really shocked me because I never had really discussed my disability. Nor were we talking about it at the time; I just never been asked that before. I was in awe of her sensitive loving compassion and mercy. It was just so genuine and real.

It was spring break of my senior year. We had gone to visit in Lafayette. Not too long before, I had written Mrs. Betty and shared with her that I was struggling with things in life. That Sunday night of our visit, Mrs. Betty came and sat down with me on the bench. She looked at me with the most gentle and caring look and said, "You said things were not going well. What's going on?"

My senior year was an emotional struggle. The very fact that Ms. Betty took the time to care to get into my heart and find out what was going on meant the world to me. I will never forget that night as she wrapped her tender loving arms around me and said, "I love you. I really do."

During my college years I kept in touch with Ms. Betty through phone calls. Being able to call Ms. Betty was such a special joy and comfort to me. She had a very special effect on me unlike anyone else. Her warm compassionate spirit ministered to me so much during my most trying years. Also I had the awesome privilege of spending time with her and Mr. Terry in their home during my visits to Lafayette. I sat and talked to Mrs. Betty for hours in her kitchen as she made her cabbage soup. Those memories will always be special to me.

Mrs. Betty's life was one of the greatest human portrayals of the deep love and compassion that God has for His people. She lived a distinguished life to exemplify the compassion of Christ that impacted so many. Yet what made her so extraordinary was her humble spirit. In one of her letters, she wrote, "Anything you felt or saw in me was God in me. Without Him I am nothing."

Whenever I need a vivid reminder of God's love for me I think about the special friendship that Mrs. Betty gave. She was my Angel from heaven that God gave me to comfort me in the deepest struggles of my life.

Transitioning Years

Transitioning from childhood to adulthood is a very vulnerable time for a person with a disability. The first 18 years of life are basically planned out with 13 years of education. The values and knowledge developed from childhood set the stage for adulthood. It is the time when desires flourish into lifelong goals that are carried out into a productive life. A person with a disability goes through the same process. We have the same desires that everyone else has.

Because high school was so rough on me emotionally, I could not bring myself to go away to college, so I lived at home. However, God moved my parents around to different states, so I moved with them. Due to the moves, I attended several colleges. Therefore, it took me seven years to complete my degree.

However, we lived in some very interesting places including Salt Lake City, UT, New Orleans, LA, and Alexanderia, LA. God provided good Christian friends in the singles groups at churches that I attended. The Christian fellowship with various friends brought joy and laughter to my life. I received my Bachelor's Degree in Business Administration from LSU in 1998.

It was during this transitional time that prejudices began to creep into every aspect of my life. Prejudice can be defined as a preconceived, unfavorable idea or opinion held with disregard to the facts that contradict it. There are a multitude of false assumptions about people with disabilities. People just assume we cannot do or perform up to full capacity in certain situations because we are different. It almost felt like that I was expected to do all of the educational work as a child. Yet society was going to put very strict limitations on the rewarding opportunities that most adults enjoy. It really feels as if people just assume that we want less in life and should be ok with less opportunity. Nothing could be further from the truth.

In adulthood, I face discrimination in many ways and in many forms. It could be walking into a restaurant with a friend and having the waitress ask my friend "What does she want?" as if I am not capable of ordering for myself. It is being denied a job and the right to work although I have a college degree. That feels like someone throwing my degree in my face and being told it is worthless because of who I am. Whenever I did work, I was treated like a second-class citizen and told some very degrading things directed toward my disability. Once again, I went to college and did all the educational work only to find out that my degree would never receive the proper respect.

These acts of discrimination are very humiliating and cut to the core of who I am. They strip me of my dignity as a person. At times it seems as if all of my strength is literally sucked out of me both mentally and physically. When I am brought to the lowest points of life, I am reminded that I am absolutely nothing without God which is exactly the point he has to bring us to in order to use us.

One night Jimmy, my husband, and I were at home. Jimmy saw his wife's heart truly broken from the darts of discrimination. He began to give me Scripture references to verses he knew that I knew for memory. One of the references he gave me was Jeremiah 29:11. So through the tears that night, I quoted, "For I know the plans that I have for you, declares the Lord. Plans for welfare and not for calamity, to give you a future and a hope." I had to cling to that verse along with other verses that he gave me just to keep from becoming utterly discouraged that everything I wanted to do in life was being hindered by discrimination.

After that conversation, a good friend named Tash Riggins called me. As we were talking, she could tell I was feeling really down. She made a very powerful statement. She said, "When you get down as far as you can go, the only way you can look is up." When she said that, I immediately thought of Psalms 121:

> *I will lift up mine eyes unto the hills, from whence cometh my help.*
>
> *My help cometh from the Lord, which made heaven and earth.*
>
> *He will not suffer thy foot to be moved: he that keepeth thee will not slumber.*
>
> *Behold, he that keepeth Israel shall neither slumber nor sleep.*
>
> *The Lord is thy keeper: the Lord is thy shade upon thy right hand.*
>
> *The sun shall not smite thee by day, nor the moon by night.*
>
> *The Lord shall preserve thee from all evil: he shall preserve thy soul.*
>
> *The Lord shall preserve thy going out and thy coming in from this time forth, and even for evermore.*

I truly identified with what David wrote in Psalm 27:13. He says, "I would have lost heart, unless I had believed that I would see the goodness of the Lord in the land of the living." It was in the midst of facing so much discrimination that God called me to start JAMIE WOMACK MINISTRIES and to publicly share my story.

Dating

Ever since I was old enough to understand the concept of dating, I knew it would be very difficult for a guy to want to date a girl with a disability. This stems from the inward struggle of fighting feelings of being inadequate or being less loveable due to my disability. When I was nine years old, I remember hearing my dad tell my older sisters when they could start dating. As he was telling them that, I remember thinking, "It's not going to matter for me, because no one will ever want me."

As I grew older, my thoughts came true. During my high school and college years, my peers had dating opportunities which I never had. At a Christian high school, we had a Junior/Senior Banquet in lieu of a prom. Dates were allowed. And yes, I was the only girl to not get asked for a date. I remember being out with friends. Dating would be the topic of discussion. Although I was laughing outwardly with people, I remember thinking to myself, "I don't know why I'm laughing. It's not for me."

A deep sense of rejection formed in my life. It felt like the whole realm of life opportunities that included dating, marriage, etc. had been taken from me. Furthermore, I knew it was because there was something about me that was harder to accept. Because God's sovereignty had been so deeply embedded in my heart as a child, blaming God was never an option. However, I did become extremely hard on myself. I basically told myself I must not be worthy of this type of love relationship. This caused several years of intense emotional turmoil in my life. There were many tears of intense hurt and frustration.

Depression became a battle for me. It was hard going through my twenties and watching people younger than me have opportunities to date and even marry. Yet it felt like I was not going to have the opportunity to choose whether I wanted to date and marry because of who I was. I felt hopeless. It was like I was living in the world where everyone was advancing to the next stage of life and yet I was blocked. No matter what I did, there always seemed to be other girls who were better. I slept just to escape the pain. It was hard to be motivated in life.

God used a friend from FBC, Lafayette named Stacey Guillory Tilley. Stacey was in the youth group when I lived in Lafayette. After I moved away, Stacey and I corresponded through letters. It was actually through letter-writing that

Stacey and I became very close friends. God was paving the way to use her greatly during one of the most trying times in my life.

As I wrestled with the dating issue, Stacey became my sounding board. She made the mental and emotional effort to put herself in my shoes and identify with what I was going through. When she did that, Stacey realized my struggle was much different and deeper than the typical girl upset because she did not have a date for that week or month.

Stacey realized it was a struggle unique to a person with a disability. It is a lifelong struggle. However, it intensifies greatly at the point of transition from childhood to adulthood. During these transitional years, societal norms begin to take over and dictate and limit opportunities for the person with a disability. And it especially cuts when it seems to define and limit relationships.

Because Stacey made this connection, it gave her the understanding and compassion to minister to me during the deepest struggles of my life. Stacey truly obeyed the biblical command found in Galatians 6:2: "Bear one another's burdens, so fulfill the law of Christ." Stacey saw me at my worst, when I was most broken. I knew that where ever I was, I could call her and say, "Stacey, life just hurts." She would patiently listen. She never condemned me or told me to get over it. Stacey truly portrayed the nurturing and compassionate nature of Christ.

One day Stacey told me that it was her mom who helped her understand the battle that I was going through. Her mom actually predicted that the dating issue would be rough on me. She described it to Stacey like this: "Jamie lives in the cage of a body that she can't control. Yet she wants all the same things that everyone else wants." Stacey's mom described it to a T.

I struggled with this for several years. One Wednesday night at the age of 26, life came to a boiling point inside of me. I had hit rock bottom emotionally. The dating issue coupled with the discrimination in other areas of life had just gotten to be too much. I had gone to get something to eat before church. While I was eating, I had a conversation with God. I said, "Lord, I can't take it anymore. I can't take the heartache and pain. I lay this at your feet. I lay it at your throne. I want to do whatever you want me to do even if it means to remain single."

At that point of surrender, I felt a huge load lifted off my shoulders. I gently heard the Lord say, "I love you. You can let yourself off the hook."

I went to church that night. Afterwards I went home. My dad walked in and said, "Do you want to meet a guy?"

I was shocked! I said yes. However in my mind I remembered the surrender that I had just made. I thought, "God, what's the deal. I just surrendered this to you."

So Dad and his friend Gary Mitchell set Jimmy and I up on a blind date the next month.

Within that month, I knew I needed God to do a work of healing in my heart. To go through years of that intense emotional turmoil, I needed God to heal my heart. He led me to read the book of Deuteronomy, which forced me to evaluate my priorities. It drives home the point that God is a very jealous God and He demands first place in our lives and rightfully so.

To describe the work that God did in me that month, I picture a banana. When you eat a banana you peel it until the only thing left standing is the part that you eat—the part that matters. During that month, God peeled everything away from my life until the only thing left standing was Him, the only thing that really matters in life.

Jamie Womack

My Miracle

The blind date was set for January 8, 2000. My parents and I went to Don's Seafood in Lecompte, LA. Bro. Gary and Elaine Mitchell came with Jimmy Womack. We all sat down to dinner, Jimmy at the end of the table. I sat next to him.

We hit it off well. I learned that Jimmy was a pastor at FBC, Maringouin. He was also the Justice of the Peace for Erwinville where he lived. I also found out that he did not drink coffee which sounded great to me because neither did I. He was a very sweet guy.

Jimmy and I lived two hours away from each other so it would be February before we would have our first date by ourselves. On a Saturday night we went to eat at the Great Wall in Baton Rouge. Of all places, he had to choose a Chinese restaurant. I do not like Chinese.

However, I was very polite and ate it. I was still checking this guy out while trying to make a good impression of myself, so eating Chinese food became tolerable for that night. It was a pleasant dinner. Afterwards, we made a hospital visit to some of the church members. I noticed his compassionate spirit toward people.

The next morning I heard Jimmy preach for the first time. His sermon really impressed me. He said very plainly that living together outside of marriage is wrong. He said it knowing that there was a couple sitting in the congregation living together in sin. That made a huge impression on me as I said to myself, "This guy is not afraid to stand up for truth and to step on anyone's toes."

In a society where many preachers choose not to preach the hard core truth of the Gospel but just want to make people feel good, Jimmy was refreshing to listen to. By the way, that couple came to Jimmy after church that day and asked him to marry them.

Jimmy's strong values impressed me. He was uncompromising on his convictions. He was the kind of guy that wasn't afraid to speak his mind. Jimmy knew what he believed in and did not waver from God's Word. He was totally against drinking and smoking. These were all of the first value criteria that I held as a Christian.

As Jimmy and I dated, I realized just how much his tenacious spirit would come into play in our relationship. At the point of my surrender, I was just really tired of the social fight altogether. In fact, part of what led me to my surrender was an eye-opening experience of the harsh truth of Proverbs 25:20 which says, "Like one who takes away a garment on a cold day, or like vinegar poured on a wound, is one who sings songs to a heavy heart." In this verse, Christians are warned of the damaging effects that a "cheer up and get over it" attitude has on someone's emotional pain.

Being on the receiving end of such an attitude during the peak of my emotional pain, I really lost the heart to trust any close relationships. My ability to trust human compassion was greatly hampered. This was a drastic change for me since I had always valued close relationships in which I felt free to share my feelings. Matthew Henry in his commentary says, "We take a wrong course if we think to relieve those in sorrow by endeavoring to make them merry." It is such a far cry from the compassionate nature of Christ that I will discuss later.[1]

Then I met Jimmy. As we started dating, I subconsciously built a wall around my heart. I was not willing to open up. I even tried to put delays in our relationship. The coldness shown toward my feelings coupled with years of self condemnation over the dating issue caused devastating effects. It really seemed as if any feelings or desire for close relationships died within my heart. During that time, God led me to the verse that says, "If your heart condemns you, God is greater than your heart."

---

1 http://www.biblegateway.com/resources/commentaries/Matthew-Henry/Prov/Proverbs-25-20

However, Jimmy knew from the start that we were meant to be together. I soon learned that he was not going anywhere. I knew it too in my head, but would not allow myself to feel it in my heart. When I would draw back in the relationship, Jimmy stood firm and persistent until I opened up to him. This showed me his strength and faith in God's will. I know God brought Jimmy into my life at a very pivotal time not only to date, but as a friend. God used Jimmy to keep me from totally closing up emotionally from relationships.

Since we lived two hours apart, weekends were the only time we could see each other. Naturally as a pastor, Jimmy often had various church ministry functions and visits on the weekend. So I participated in different ministry functions as well as visits to get to know the church members. Ladies of the church opened their home for me to stay. As we dated, we both learned that ministry was the heartbeat that we shared.

As I watched Jimmy interact with his church members, I saw a guy who loved people. He never met a stranger. He loved to laugh with them and just have a good time. His caring spirit was evident to all. What you see is what you get with Jimmy. He was definitely a down to earth guy who was genuine and real. Jimmy's fun loving spirit and authentic attitude toward life was what endeared him to many, including me.

On Saturday, July 22, 2000, Jimmy took me to his church. It was just the two of us. I sat on the first pew. Jimmy got down on one knee and asked me to marry him! Knowing that it was God's will, I said "Yes!" We were both thrilled that God had led us to that point. We went out on the lake to eat at Satterfield's Restaurant to celebrate!

January 13, 2001, was our wedding day!!

It was perfect in every way. We were married at Donahue Baptist Church in Pineville, LA. Many of our relatives came from different states. Several Lafayette friends came, including Ms. Betty and Mr. Terry. Stacey was my matron of honor. Family and friends made up the bridesmaids and groomsmen. Basically, all of Erwinville showed up on Jimmy's side. The ushers told me they stopped counting people at 200.

The support was overwhelming. There is nothing more satisfying than to stand at the altar at my wedding and knowing beyond a shadow of a doubt that I was marrying the man God had chosen for me.

We had three ministers. Bro. James Greer, who was my pastor at Donahue, officiated our wedding. Bro. Gary Mitchell definitely had to have a part since he was involved in starting this relationship. And then, of course my dad. I wanted Dad to concentrate on being my dad that day rather than being the main minister. But he did take part by doing the Lord's Supper with Jimmy and me during the ceremony.

Jimmy is truly my miracle. God has blessed me with an awesome Christian husband! He brings so much laughter and joy to my life. One thing that meant so much to me was the fact that my disability has never been an issue in our relationship. Since Jimmy met me, he accepted me for who I am. He also recognized the fact that my disability did not enter my conversation as an excuse or a crutch. I just lived life and found ways to do things that may be more difficult for me. I liked how Jimmy naturally knew the times I needed help and just chimed in not making any kind of issue about it. This showed tremendous respect toward my independence.

Most of all, he loves the Lord and preaches the truth! He truly has a pastor's heart. Since Jimmy is a bi-vocational pastor, he is also a hospice chaplain. I see God using his chaplain job as an extension of his ministerial gifts. It takes a special person to constantly deal with people in their dying moments. Jimmy has that gift that stems from the example of Christ Himself. During His earthly ministry, Jesus purposely put Himself in the way of hurting people to bring comfort.

Sacred Right Stolen

Sacred rights are those God-given rights that are interwoven into the very heart of humanity. The heart is the very center of human emotion and innermost feelings. It is that from which the well-springs of life flow. Certain rights are considered sacred because they are heart-felt desires created by God Himself. These rights were beautifully hand-crafted into desires through the fabric of human emotion. They have a purpose that was set in stone since the beginning of Creation.

God created Adam to have fellowship with Him. He saw that Adam was lonely so he created Eve to be his help-mate. He then told them to be fruitful and multiply. Thus the family unit was specifically designed by God as a holy entity. It involved human desire as expressed through the loneliness of man and the love between a man and a woman. It is considered sacred because it is a God-designed relational unit in which human emotion was used to incorporate God's purpose.

Having a baby is one of those sacred rights and desires that are embedded into every girl's heart. It is every little girl's dream to grow up, get married, and have kids. I have already shared my struggle with the dating issue. Because of that, I never really allowed myself to have those dreams. I subconsciously denied myself access to those feelings and dreams. When I began to date Jimmy I felt like I had access to these dreams that everyone else had had since their childhood.

As a child, I enjoyed holding babies and playing with them. I remember taking the Sears catalog and looking at the baby section just for amusement. When we got older and Stacey had her babies, I remember carrying them around her house since they were newborns. She saw the joy on my face as I rocked one of them to sleep. Stacey gave me the upmost respect with her children.

Once Jimmy and I started dating and talking about marriage, it began to dawn on me for the first time in my life that I was going to actually have a right to have a baby! I remember discussing with Jimmy about trying to have one child and then we would go from there. Even in that discussion, my disability was not an issue to Jimmy. We both wondered if my body could handle pregnancy from a medical standpoint. So we would see what God had planned.

Unfortunately, the freedom to just enjoy the thought of having my own child did not last long. I would soon learn just how low and degrading societal views can be toward people with disabilities. I heard some very demeaning statements such as a "a baby's life would be in danger under your care," and "I've never seen a person with cerebral palsy be the primary caretaker of a baby," and "You would need counseling if you have kids." I was in total shock that people actually thought they had a right to tell me these things because they were "normal."

Furthermore, I was treated differently around children. I was not seen as a respectable adult. In many instances, I was made to feel incapable of holding a baby and was treated like a child. This was very insulting, especially after Stacey had given me the complete freedom to carry her babies. I remember going to comfort a child when another adult moved ahead of me to do it. People really thought my disability prevented me from holding and caring for a precious baby. This was extremely frustrating and humiliating.

The sad part is that complete strangers treated me with more respect than people who knew me. We were taking pictures at church one weekend and I was helping the people as they came in. A grandmother came in with her 9-month old grandson. The lady sat down and looked very tired, so I offered to take her grandbaby to the room where they were taking pictures. Without hesitation she allowed me to do that.

That woman will never know what that simple act of respect meant to me. Interestingly, a lady from our church saw me carrying the baby and commented to Jimmy, "Jamie is really good with babies."

One of the most sacred places of my heart had been defiled and destroyed. That right that had been formed by God in my heart and complemented by human emotion was trampled on by deliberate insults with no respect toward my feelings. Since it was a right given by God, it was defilement of His authority in my life. It was as if I was hearing, "We don't care how you feel or what you can do. You just can't care for a baby because you are handicapped." Now I had no rights to my feelings or abilities.

To do this to a disabled woman who has fought and conquered countless obstacles in life, literally destroys every sense of self worth and dignity. The insults and discriminatory acts toward the baby issue terrified me. I lost all my self confidence in doing something that I know I was capable of doing. I feared that if I had a baby that someone would take it away or that people would be hovering over me and not allow me the freedom to take care of my child. The heartache and pain that these insults have caused has been indescribable. I just never knew people could be so mean and brutal to the heart and soul of a person with a disability.

How very true are the words of Proverbs 18:21 which says, "Death and life are in the power of the tongue, and those who love it will eat its fruits." The truth of this verse was really brought to light one day in Sunday School. The lesson was on the power of words. Our Sunday School teacher had an awesome illustration. She brought a brick and passed it around to everyone. As each of us held it, the heaviness of the brick was noted. One of the ladies held it and solemnly said, "Wow, I could do a lot of damage with this, but I could also build a shelter."

The weight of words can be paralleled to the weight of the brick. They weigh heavily on the hearts of the receiver either to build up or tear down. And thus, the degrading comments were a heavy weight and did great damage to my heart.

My doctor was a Christian and had the foresight to handle this situation very delicately. He did tell me that I would be able to have kids. However, he pulled Jimmy to the side to talk to him. The doctor told Jimmy that although I could have kids, it would be very rough on my body. The doctor said he did not want to break my heart and tell me not to have kids. He could tell that my heart had already been crushed over this issue. He laid the risks out and left the decision up to us.

Jimmy's strength was great. He focused on the medical risks of pregnancy. He feared for my life. I also was very nervous about it being rough on my body. That, coupled with the emotional trauma of the insults, caused me to become very frail emotionally. Without having to deal with the hostility of societal views, there was a slight chance that I might have tried to have a child. But the emotional weight of both medical issues and societal issues was too much. Fortunately, Jimmy was not the type that he just had to have kids. After a couple of years of marriage, we decided not to have kids, knowing that God had ministry as our primary life focus.

In all honesty, I probably would not have attempted pregnancy due to medical concerns. However, the degradation made it extremely painful. I will always wonder what it would have been like to have the freedom to have a child without fearing the insults. In reading this, I hope people will realize that people with disabilities have desires and feelings just like anyone else, and we know our capabilities without others questioning them. All we ask is to be treated with equal respect.

It is amazing how God shows His unfailing love in the small things. Our deacon's wife is in charge of getting the Mother's Day gifts for all the mothers of the church. She has had no idea of the heart wrenching struggle this issue has been for me. Yet she has always given me a gift, recognizing me as the "mother of the church" as the pastor's wife. Our God is so faithful to minister to us.

A couple of years ago, I spoke at FBC, Broussard, LA. As I was walking out to my car after church, a man started talking to me. He asked if I had kids. I said no. He continued by saying, "I bet you wanted them." I nodded my head in agreement. That really touched me because he acknowledged that I had a right to desire to have children and did not automatically assume that I was incapable.

That man showed me tremendous respect and dignity in that area of life.

Recently, I talked to a lady who said she knew a couple in which both the man and the woman had cerebral palsy. She said that they too faced the insults. But they defied the odds and had a beautiful son. This made my heart happy for them. I also realized that upon hearing this, that God had given a peace and fulfillment in my calling to JWM.

Jamie Womack Ministries

December, 2012, marked the 10-year anniversary of JAMIE WOMACK MINISTRIES. When God called me to this ministry, I was also involved in doing discipleship training work for our Association. It was what God used to fuel the fire within me to have a passion to lead others to a deeper commitment to discipleship. Thus, the mission statement was formed.

JWM Mission Statement: JWM seeks to encourage people to view their trials in life as opportunities to draw closer to God and become more intimate with him. It also seeks to encourage people to lay their trials at God's throne. For in doing so, God is able to take those same trials and turn them into tools of ministry for His honor and His Glory.

Over the years I have seen growth in many aspects of the ministry. Beginning with my presentation, God has impressed me to go deeper into the heartfelt struggles of people with disabilities. Through that, I am able to inter-twine with the principles of God's grace, compassion, and forgiveness into all areas of life.

In 2004, I spoke in the three morning services at FBC, Covington, LA. They asked me for a title to my testimony. Thus, the title "A Call to Surrender" was originated. Building on that title, God led me to a song called "The Altar" by Charles Billingsley. I now use it as the invitation song. It talks about laying things down at the altar so that our gift of service can be pure before our King.

I still had a longing to work and use my education. From 2007-2010, I worked as a Jr. High Teacher at a Christian school. When that job ended, I went on several job interviews. I did not have one job offer. To a college graduate who has a burning desire to work and be productive in life, this is very humiliating.

On January 23, 2011, I was scheduled to speak at FBC, Melbourne, Florida, in their two morning services before a thousand people. Jimmy and I had planned to make it our anniversary trip. The week before, the truth that Satan throws the most obstacles in our way when God wants to do one of His greatest works came alive. The Sunday before, Jimmy got really sick with bronchitis and had to go into the hospital. I knew that he would not be able to make the trip, so I texted my best friend Stacey to see if she could go with me. She said she would talk to her husband and let me know.

On Monday morning Jimmy was miserably sick. He had some medical tests scheduled for Tuesday. We were talking and I mentioned I would wait until after the tests on Tuesday and make a decision about whether or not to re-schedule. Even in his misery, he immediately said with bold-ness and authority, "The decision has already been made. You are going!" At that point I still had not heard back from Stacey, but I knew God would make a way. Shortly after that, Stacey confirmed to go.

That Monday night I came down with a bad cold and cough. I had to go home and take care of myself. On the way home I stopped by Urgent Care and told the doctor to give me whatever he could because I had to speak before 1,000 people that next Sunday!

Jimmy's parents helped by being there with Jimmy for the tests. I was able to stay home and rest. His mom assured me that she would keep a close eye on Jimmy while I was gone. That relieved a lot of stress. His tests came back clear and he came home that Wednesday.

The pastor at FBC, Melbourne, called Tuesday night. He was Bro. Larry Bazer whom I had known since a child. His wife, Gayle, had seen my posts on *Facebook* and they won-dered if I was still coming. I told Bro. Larry about Jimmy's authoritative statement and said, "Bro. Larry, you have my word. I will be there at FBC, Melbourne Sunday morning.

I was better by Friday although my physical strength was still not up to par. Stacey was so great that weekend.

She made it her mission to stand by me and to make life easier on me. She knew the great stress I had been under. I fully intended for us to split the 14 hour drive. She offered several times to drive even when it was my turn. Stacey later told me that when I took her up on offers to drive she knew I wasn't feeling well. She knows I love to drive and would have done so if I had felt better.

We made it and had an awesome experience. We went out to eat after the services on Sunday with the Bazers. Gayle told me that there was a couple there that day who had just learned that their son would never go beyond an 11-year-old mental capacity. They were devastated and were desperate to know that God still works in the most difficult circumstances. Wow! Talk about divine appointment! It made me so grateful for Jimmy's authoritative statement about going and the imperative to keep focused on the calling of God, even when it seems that everything is falling apart.

It was after that trip that God called me to lay down once and for all my desire to work in the secular world and to launch JWM full time. When I told Jimmy about God's calling to JWM full time, he simply said, "Go!" We are to go at the call of the Almighty God. As soon as I did that, God began to open doors left and right. I spoke twenty times in six different states in 2011. In 2012 I spoke forty-one times in six different states. We serve an awesome God and He will prevail over Satan's obstacles!!!

As I have written about the past years, Philippians 1:6 comes to mind: "And I am sure of this, he who began a good work in you will bring it to completion at the day of Jesus Christ." I look forward to see what God does in the future of JWM!

Guard Your Heart

"Above all else, guard your heart, for it is the wellspring of life." Proverbs 4:23.

This verse came to life in me as I thought about why discrimination is so painful and leaves life-long scars. Discrimination is a direct trampling and demolishing of the desires of the heart. When it is compared to the fact that "it is the wellsprings of life," it made me realize that discrimination literally deadens the life cells of the heart. It travels throughout the different stages of life and centers around relating to society.

For instance, as a child, to be liked and accepted is the primary desire. To face teasing and shunning sent negative thoughts to my brain. I remember wrestling with thoughts like, "I must not be good enough for people."

As I grew older, the wrestling with those thoughts increased as the teasing turned into the reality of rejection of life opportunities such as employment. Discrimination cuts the deepest when it seems to define and limit the types of relationships we are to have in life. I really thought that when I surrendered the dating issue and God brought Jimmy into my life, the worst was over. Then to be literally degraded about the baby issue destroyed my heart.

Since my desires were so degraded, I lost the ability to respect my feelings. It became difficult for me to feel gentleness and compassion toward my innermost feelings. My heart felt numb. Therefore, I emotionally further shut down my desire to cultivate any real close friendships. After we married, I made several good friends around our church and our community who enriched my life greatly. But I put up a guard around my innermost heart. God used Jimmy as my stronghold as he saw my hidden pain.

I saw growth in my ministry in several areas. Even in my presentation, I saw God gradually incorporate the principles of forgiveness as I went through the process of forgiveness myself. In fact, I received a letter from a 17-year old boy who told me that he realized his need to forgive. God's work was evident during the first eight years of JWM. However, it would not be until 2010 that God would begin preparing my heart to launch into JWM full-time.

On January 2, 2010, God would use my Angel Betty to bring a defining moment of His grace and compassion.

Jamie Womack

Jimmy and I went that day to FBC, Lafayette, to be with Mrs. Betty for Mr. Terry's funeral. We stood in line leading up to Mrs. Betty. When she saw me, the surprise and joy on her face was priceless!

What she did after we embraced made a lasting impression. She took the time to put her Kleenex down so that she could have both hands. As she cupped my face with her hands, I felt that deep warm gentle compassion go right through my heart. At that moment, the numbness to compassion toward my innermost feelings began to crumble. How ironic that God would bring me back to the one person that He has always used to minister that deep gentleness and compassion toward my innermost feelings.

We sat through the funeral. As the family walked out behind the casket, Mrs. Betty spotted me and reached out for my hand. We grasped hands. I knew in my heart that was meant for a sign of our special friendship. In our phone conversation two weeks later, she brought that moment up and confirmed my thoughts.

She said, "Notice you were the only one I talked to as I walked out behind the casket. That's because you are my special girl."

I told her that night that I would come see her soon. My full intent was to go see her and tell her the incredible impact she had made on my life. However, that phone call would be the last time I would speak to my Precious Angel

Betty. She passed away January 29, 2010, just one month after her beloved husband.

Although I never made that intended visit, I know that Mrs. Betty knew my heart. For when we grasped hands at Mr. Terry's funeral, we had the same thought of our special friendship on our hearts and minds without even speaking it. That is something that only true genuine friends experience. Even in the midst of sadness, God used Mrs. Betty to shower His compassion and grace and to give me a deeper understanding of how He wants to crown His people with love and compassion.

The heart is the most volatile place for human emotion. When my feelings seem to be railroaded by the world through discrimination, it becomes very meaningful to know that God values my heart so much that He gave the command to "guard your heart." Even as I was writing this book, God enabled me to share for the first time my struggle with the baby issue. It showed me that God will provide ways for us to express and validate our feelings without being offensive to others. As the numbness toward my innermost feelings began to crumble, it enabled me to experience God's grace and compassion in a real and powerful way. For it is within the heart that God does His work of cleansing and purification.

Ephesians 3:14-19 says, "For this reason, I bow my knees before the Father, from whom every family in heaven and on earth is named, that according to the riches of his glory he may grant you to be strengthened with power through his Spirit in your inner being, so that Christ may dwell in your hearts through faith—that you being rooted and grounded in love, may have strength to comprehend with all the saints what is the breadth and length and height and depth, and to know the love of Christ that surpasses knowledge, that you may be filled with all the fullness of God."

As God did His work of compassion in my heart, He strengthened my testimony. I began to speak about my Angel Betty and my friend Stacey and their real Christ-like compassion. Compassion, grace, forgiveness, and mercy became my focal points. These are the very principles that apply to situations in all walks of life.

Redemption Rooted in the Heart of Compassion

To fully understand the compassion in God's character, we must look at the emotions of Jesus Himself that he portrayed in His earthly ministry. Jesus was a very emotional person. And He was very open about it.

Different situations aroused different emotions in Jesus. He was moved with compassion when people were hurting. He was angry in the Temple when it was being misused. Jesus gently rebuked the sin of the woman caught in adultery. He grieved at Lazurus' death. He agonized in the Garden of Gethsemane as he was approaching the crucifixion. Jesus' display of human emotion is such a powerful portrayal of the relational attribute in the human race.

Having a real sense of Jesus' identification with every human emotion enables us to grasp an understanding of

His concern for our feelings. Hebrews 4:15-16 says, "For we do not have a high priest who is unable to empathize with our weaknesses, but we have one who has been tempted in every way, just as we are—yet he did not sin. Let us then approach God's throne of grace with confidence, so that we may receive mercy and find grace to help us in our time of need."

These verses encompass the concept of how very real Jesus' feelings are. I love how 1 Peter 5:10 parallels faith in God alongside of our suffering. "In his kindness God called you to share in his eternal glory by means of Christ Jesus. So after you have suffered a little while, he will restore, support, and strengthen you, and he will place you on a firm foundation." God values our feelings and cares about our suffering.

Once we understand His compassion, we are able to better understand the grace and mercy that led Him to the cross. Redemption was rooted in God's heart of compassion. John 3:16 says, "For God so loved the world that he gave his one and only Son, that whoever believes in him shall not perish but have eternal life." It was the love and compassion of God that was carried out through His Son as a living sacrifice for all of mankind. In turn, that gives us strength to exemplify those same redemptive qualities as we obey the Biblical command to forgive those who trespass against us.

The Christian duty to forgive is plain in Ephesians 4:31-32: "Let all bitterness and wrath and anger and clamor and slander be put away from you, along with malice. Be kind to one another, tender-hearted, forgiving one another, as God in Christ forgave you."

How did Christ forgive us? 1 John 1:9 says, "If we confess our sins, he is faithful and just and will forgive us our sins and purify us from all unrighteousness." Psalms 103:12 says, "as far as the east is from the west, so far has he removed our transgressions from us." Once we go to Christ for forgiveness, He no longer holds our sins against us. Nor should we hold the offenses of others against them.

If you have noticed, nowhere in the book do I name anyone who has offended me. I do not even mention my high school nor do I list it on my Facebookpage. This is out of pure respect and love for the people. It is also in accordance to the biblical command to "let all slander be put away from you." True forgiveness is not wanting to damage someone's reputation. Jesus demonstrated this very principle as He faced rejection.

Luke 9:51-56 tells about the time a Samaritan village rejected our Savior. "Now it came to pass, when the time had come for Him to be received up, that He steadfastly set His face to go to Jerusalem, and sent messengers before His face. And as they went, they entered a village of Samaritans, to prepare for Him.

But they did not receive Him because His face was set for the journey to Jerusalem. And when His disciples James and John saw this, they said, 'Lord, do you want us to command fire to come down from heaven and consume them, just as Elijah did?' But He turned and rebuked them, and said, 'You do not know what manner of spirit you are of. For the Son of Man did not come to destroy men's lives but to save them.' And they went to another village."

A couple a years ago a former high school classmate messaged me on *Facebook*. This person had read an excerpt of my testimony which included my experience in high school, and questioned me about what went on in high school.

This was my response: As far as what happened in high school, some things were ongoing. I think it was obvious. However, it was twenty years ago, and I have put it behind me. The only thing I'll say is look at my nickname in our senior yearbook—that might jog your memory. I do believe a lot of it was done in joking. However, it did have a great effect on me emotionally.

But I'm not going to name anyone out of respect and because it was twenty years ago. Do I hold any grudges? Absolutely not! In fact, back in 2001, after I was married, I had a long phone conversation with one of our classmates that was involved. Nothing was ever said about it. We just had a great talk about life. They probably never even thought about what happened and the effect it had on me. We've all matured and gone on, living our lives for the praise and glory of our precious Lord and Savior.

It is when we are called on to forgive someone ourselves that we reveal the depth of our understanding and appreciation of what Jesus did for us on the cross. To have an unforgiving heart basically tramples on the meaning of the cross as if to say it was not enough. An unforgiving spirit leaves no room for redemption because it stems from an uncompassionate heart. For Jesus paid the price once and for all to redeem all of mankind out of His heart of compassion.

Finding True Dignity

We live in a very class-oriented society. People are put into first, second, or third class according to income and prestige. Greater value is placed on the richest. Competition and prestige rule the world. Everyone is out to make a name for themselves. Recognition is given to the best looking and the most competitive. This stirs up selfish desires to race to the top. Unfortunately, respect for others is often forfeited.

This worldly mind-set has invaded much of the Christian atmosphere. Power and recognition mixed with a little spirituality creates pride and arrogance. A pious and judgmental attitude is formed and aimed at people who may "look" lower class and automatically deemed less spiritual. For the person with a disability, the Christian atmosphere that was a safe haven becomes an extension of the battle ground for respect and acceptance.

A newspaper reporter once asked me, "What is the hardest thing about your disability?" She quickly put her pencil down and gave me a look of utter total shock when I answered, "discrimination." A pastor friend of mine described to his congregation as being despised by the world. That is really how it feels. Lo and behold, God addresses this very issue in His Word.

God gives his view of discrimination in very simple terms. Acts 10:34 says, "And Peter opened his mouth and said, 'Of a truth I perceive that God is no respecter of persons.'" I think it is very interesting that this verse starts out with "Of a truth," emphasizing the truthfulness of God's view. In fact, God considers partiality to be such an insult that he compares it to blaspheming His Name.

James 2:1-10, says, "My brethren, have not the faith of our Lord Jesus Christ, [the Lord] of glory, with respect of persons. For if there come unto your assembly a man with a gold ring, in goodly apparel, and there come in also a poor man in vile raiment; And ye have respect to him that weareth the gay clothing, and say unto him, Sit thou here in a good place; and say to the poor, Stand thou there, or sit here under my footstool: Are ye not then partial in yourselves, and are become judges of evil thoughts? Hearken, my beloved brethren, Hath not God chosen the poor of this world rich in faith, and heirs of the kingdom which he hath promised to them that love him? But ye have despised the poor. Do not rich men oppress you, and draw you before the judgment seats? Do not they blaspheme that worthy name by the which ye are called? If ye fulfil the royal law according to the scripture, Thou shalt love thy neighbour as thyself, ye do well: But if ye have respect to persons, ye commit sin, and are convinced of the law as transgressors. For whosoever shall keep the whole law, and yet offend in one [point], he is guilty of all."

It is ironic that the people who are looked down upon by the world are the very ones that God chooses to display His Glory in such a way that all human boasting and recognition becomes null and void. "But God has chosen the foolish things of the world to put to shame the wise, and God has chosen the weak things of the world to put to shame the things that are mighty; and the base things and the things which are despised God has chosen, and the things which are not, to bring to nothing the things that are, that no flesh should glory in His presence." 1 Corinthians 1:27-29

So, the question arises, "Where does one find true dignity and value when the world has striped it away?"

Psalms 62:7 says, "In God is my salvation and glory; The rock of my strength, And my refuge is in God." God so eloquently defines the tremendous value that HE has for His people. "But you are a chosen generation, a royal priesthood, a holy nation, His own special people, that you may proclaim the praises of Him who called you out of darkness into His marvelous light." 1 Peter 2:9

On October 7, 2012, I spoke at New Day Fellowship in Eureka Springs, AR. It was a spirit-filled service. After I spoke, the pastor made an interesting analogy to the surrenders that I shared. He used my college degree as an example and reviewed the fact that God called me to lay that down at the altar. In this day and age, a college degree is highly valued and gives a person somewhat of an upper edge on prestige and self-dignity. The pastor paralleled it to the truth found in Luke 9:24, "For whosoever will save his life shall lose it: but whosoever will lose his life for my sake, the same shall save it."

To find true value and dignity, we must do the exact opposite of how the world defines it. According to the world, we are to grab all we can to ensure success. We are to demand our rights. Yet the biblical view of true dignity is a life of surrender and humble submission to our Lord and Savior. Jesus Himself gives His definition of success is found in the Sermon on the Mount in Matthew 5:2-12:

> Then He opened His mouth and taught them,
> saying:
> Blessed are the poor in spirit, For theirs is the
> kingdom of heaven.
> Blessed are those who mourn, For they shall be
> comforted.
> Blessed are the meek, For they shall inherit the
> earth.
> Blessed are those who hunger and thirst for
> righteousness, For they shall be filled.
> Blessed are the merciful, For they shall obtain
> mercy.

Blessed are the pure in heart, For they shall see God.

Blessed are the peacemakers, For they shall be called sons of God.

Blessed are those who are persecuted for righteousness' sake, For theirs is the kingdom of heaven.

Blessed are you when they revile and persecute you, and say all kinds of evil against you falsely for My sake. Rejoice and be exceedingly glad, for great is your reward in heaven, for so they persecuted the prophets who were before you.

The lesson I learned is that when we lose our life that is when we truly find it.

Jamie Womack

Trial to Tools

Several years ago, I was flying on a airplane. I just happened to sit by a man who claimed to be a preacher. We got into an interesting theological discussion. He said to me, "If you had enough faith in God, he could heal you right now." Apparently he thought I must not have a strong faith since I was disabled. My response was, "Yes, I know God can heal me, but I also know that God can receive glory through my handicap."

This guy's philosophy reveals one of the prevailing beliefs in our society today. There are Christians that believe that once you are saved, God wants you to have perfect health and wealth. And if you do not have perfect health and wealth, you are just not spiritual enough. It is a part of the prosperity gospel.

I just have one major problem with the prosperity gospel belief. It is not in God's Word!! Looking at the life of

Christ, the whole reason He came to this earth was to suffer and die the most gruesome death on the cross, which for us resulted in the ultimate reward of eternal life. Likewise it the times of suffering in our lives that often create the pathways to our experiencing God's amazing love and grace in the most life-changing ways.

Even the great men of the Bible struggled greatly and grew spiritually. In 2 Corinthians 12, the apostle Paul tells of his thorn in the flesh. He even begs three times for it to be taken away. But Jesus simply responds, "My grace is sufficient for you, for my power is made perfect in weakness." Paul then continues by saying, "Therefore I will boast all the more gladly about my weaknesses, so that Christ's power may rest on me. That is why, for Christ's sake, I delight in weaknesses, in insults, in hardships, in persecutions, in difficulties. For when I am weak, then I am strong."

When trials come our way, it should be of no surprise. Jesus said that we would have trouble. John 16:33 says, "I have told you these things, so that in me you may have peace. In this world you will have trouble. But take heart! I have overcome the world."

James 1:2-4 says, "Consider it pure joy, my brothers, whenever you face trials of many kinds, because you know that the testing of your faith develops perseverance. Perseverance must finish its work so that you may be mature and complete, not lacking anything.

It has been through the struggles of life that I have been able to experience God's love and power in incredible ways. Invaluable friendships have developed out of both my emotional and physical struggles. Mrs. Betty's warm gentle compassion looked good during the year I had shut down socially. As I struggled with the dating issue, Stacey's encouragement and understanding became a stronghold for me.

Because it takes me longer to write, I always had to have a note taker in school. My first day of college in my algebra class, the professor announced that I would need a note taker. The girl who responded was named Tash Riggins. After class, Tash and I went to the student union to get to know each other. We quickly learned that we were both Christians. On that day, God provided a two-fold need—a note taker and a good Christian friend on a public college campus. Tash is a life-long friend.

There is a reason for everything that happens in life. Jesus even gives the specific reason why people have disabilities. John 9:2-3 says, "And His disciples asked Him, 'Rabbi, who sinned, this man or his parents, that he would be born blind?' Jesus answered, 'It was neither that this man sinned, nor his parents; but it was so that the works of God might be displayed in him....'"

We can hold on to the promise in Romans 8:28 that says, "And we know that all things work together for good to them that love God and to those who are called according to his purpose." The key words are "all things." The truth of this verse reveals the Sovereignty of God in both the good and the bad. It also reveals the desire of God to work good even in the tough situations.

When trials come our way, we are faced with the choice of either becoming bitter or better people. It is human nature to become disgruntled when we face the unfairness of life. When people hurt us, a war emerges within us as we wrestle between anger and bitterness and forgiveness and love. This war is described in Ephesians 6:12: "For we wrestle not against flesh and blood, but against principalities, against powers, against the rulers of the darkness of this world, against spiritual wickedness in high places." It all boils down to human nature versus a surrendered life to Jesus Christ.

For it is within a surrendered life that we find purpose for the heart-wrenching times of life. The Bible says, "Let nothing be wasted." John 6:12 I firmly believe that no heartache is wasted without meaning. There is always a spiritual lesson to be learned. It is the tough times of life that force us to rely on God and to press for that truth of knowing that His ways are higher than our ways. God longs to draw us unto Himself and to let us know that He is truly our Sufficiency. In turn, God is willing and able to turn each trial in life into a tool of ministry for His honor and His glory.

It is a life of faith, not of reason or intellect, but a life of knowing who makes us "go."

The root of faith is the knowledge of a Person, and one of the biggest snares is the idea that God is sure to lead us to success.[2]

Many battles have been fought inside the chambers of my heart. Yet it has been through the unseen battle scars that God has taught me about His grace, faithfulness, compassion, and forgiveness. All along God was preparing the testimonial message of "A Call to Surrender." I integrate these fundamental issues as God gives me the grace to speak about the most heartbreaking times of my life. These same issues enable people of all walks of life to be reached as they hear how these Godly principles can be applied to the toughest circumstances. JWM has touched many kinds of people such as:

- former drug addict
- alcoholic
- parents who just learned that their 11-year-old son would not go beyond an 11-year-old mental capacity
- a 17-year-old boy who realized the need to forgive
- A mother of a special needs child coming to salvation

_____
2 Chambers, Oswald. <u>My Utmost For His Highest</u>. Barbour & Company, Inc., 1935, page 79.

One of the most touching moments of ministry came after speaking on a Sunday night in Alabama. A man came up and said that he brought a friend that night whom he had been trying to get to come to church. As they walked out his friend told him, "I really needed to hear what she had to say tonight." The man choked up as he looked at me and said, "Thank you for your ministry."

I thank God for His Sovereign hand leading me to present my testimony in such a way that He can reach and draw people to Himself. I am nothing without God and am humbled to be used as an instrument in His Kingdom.

My life story can attest to the truth found in the lyrics of the Steven Curtis Chapman's song, *My Redeemer is Faithful and True.*

As I look back on the road I've travelled,
I see so many times He carried me through;
And if there's one thing that I've learned in my life,
My Redeemer is faithful and true.
My Redeemer is faithful and true.

My Redeemer is faithful and true.
Everything He has said He will do,
And every morning His mercies are new.
My Redeemer is faithful and true.

My heart rejoices when I read the promise

Jamie Womack

'There is a place I am preparing for you.'
I know someday I'll see my Lord face to face,
'Cause my Redeemer is faithful and true.
My Redeemer is faithful and true.
My Redeemer is faithful and true.
Everything He has said He will do,
And every morning His mercies are new.
My Redeemer is faithful and true.

And in every situation He has proved His love to me;
When I lack the understanding, He gives more grace to me.

My Redeemer is faithful and true.
Everything He has said He will do,
And every morning His mercies are new.
My Redeemer is faithful and true.

This book would not be complete until I shared how you can know my Eternal Hope—Jesus Christ. Below is the *Plan of Salvation* that illustrates why we are in need of a Savior. All you have to do is pray the sinner's prayer and ask Jesus to come into your heart.

Plan of Salvation: Sin Separates you from God

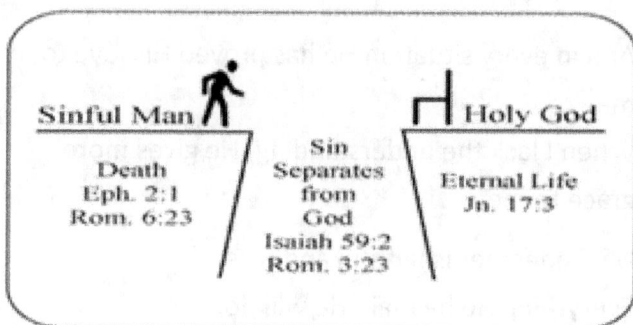

```
Sinful Man 🚶         🕇 Holy God

  Death          Sin         Eternal Life
  Eph. 2:1    Separates        Jn. 17:3
  Rom. 6:23      from
                 God
              Isaiah 59:2
              Rom. 3:23
```

Good Works, Religion, & Morality can't save you

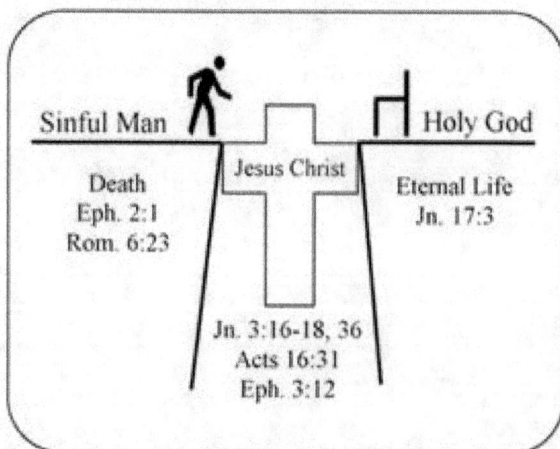

```
Sinful Man 🚶              🕇 Holy God

  Death       Jesus Christ    Eternal Life
  Eph. 2:1                      Jn. 17:3
  Rom. 6:23


              Jn. 3:16-18, 36
                Acts 16:31
                Eph. 3:12
```

Only Jesus Christ can Save you.

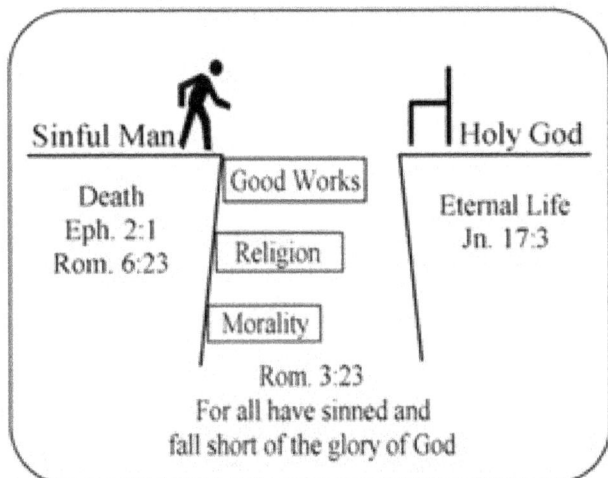

Sinful Man — Holy God

Death
Eph. 2:1
Rom. 6:23

Good Works

Religion

Morality

Eternal Life
Jn. 17:3

Rom. 3:23
For all have sinned and
fall short of the glory of God

Sinner's Prayer

Dear Lord Jesus,

I realize that I am a sinner and have fallen short of your Glory. I believe that you died on the cross for my sin. Please forgive me of my sins. Come into my heart and be Lord and Savior of my life. Thank you dear Jesus for hearing my prayer. In Jesus' Name, Amen

Testimony

"Hello, I am Payton Lippert, an 11th grade girl in the youth group at Westwood Baptist Church. When you shared your testimony, God broke me. I have been saved for about 5 years and strive to live for God in all aspects of life.

Lately, I have dealt with normal high school issues that have made me apathetic in worship and service to my Lord and Savior.

As you shared your story, God, as plain as day, renewed my passion of how awesome He is! I poured my heart out at the altar and just laid everything inside of me at His throne.

I woke up this morning excited and genuinely passionate about the cause of Jesus Christ!

I just want to finish by saying how much of a light you are!

Thank you for your ministry and being willing to follow Jesus Christ in surrendering everything. What a testimony and role model that was and is to me! God is good all the time! Thank you for being like a light bulb and not showing the glass, but displaying the light inside.

I felt led to share this with you as you continue your ministry in sharing and serving for the cause of Jesus Christ."

Your sister in Christ,

Payton Lippert

www.ingramcontent.com/pod-product-compliance
Lightning Source LLC
LaVergne TN
LVHW021134080426
835509LV00010B/1354